Prolance

www.prolancewriting.com
California, USA
© 2019 Mariam Saad

ISBN: 978-1-7338267-4-7

Trilingual Sofia

BOOK 1

Eid Breakfast at Abuela's

Written by Mariam Saad
Illustrated by Chaymaa Sobhy

Dedication:

Simply and intricately the
most beautiful flower in existence.
Delicate and strong. Patient and decisive.
Supportive. Encouraging. Impossibly selfless.
Hishmat, Mom, you are always at the start of
everything wonderful in my life.

My name is Sofia and Ramadan this año was very special.

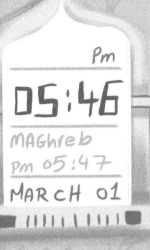

It was the first time that I tried to fast.

I drank **agua** and had some snacks in the morning and afternoon, and then fasted for the last two hours of each day.

Even though Mama's family does not celebrate Ramadan or Eid, my **abuela** prepared an Eid breakfast for Mama, Baba, and me for the first time.

To get to Abuela's we flew in an **avión** across the country. We left for the airport right after we broke our last fast.

Mama brought my scrapbook on the airplane so we could work on it during the long flight. She keeps memorable things there to remind us of my childhood. It has pictures of me learning to walk and the first **cuchara** that I ever ate with. I used it to eat plain white yogurt sprinkled with tiny black raisins.

Before I fell asleep for the night flight, I had finished my **bolsa** of pretzels and taped it to the page about Eid in my scrapbook.

"Wake up Raheem. Buenos días Sofia," before I knew it, the airplane had landed and Mama was waking Baba and me up to get ready for Eid prayer. We used the bathroom on the airplane to brush our teeth and change into our Eid clothes.

I wore my new **ropa**: a long blue dress with orange sleeves and flowers at the bottom.

After we prayed and met our **amigos** at the mosque...

...we drove to Abuela's for **desayuno**.

"Clara, Raheem, and Sofia! I have missed you **mis hijos**," Abuela said to us when we arrived at her **casa**. We each greeted her with a big hug and a kiss on the cheek.

To my surprise, she had invited my tíos, tías, and cousins all to enjoy an Eid breakfast with us.

I am the youngest of my cousins on Mama's side of the family, and also the only one learning **tres** languages.

When I told Abuela that I knew the entire alphabet in English, Arabic, and Spanish she lifted me up into the air and spun me around.

Abuela had me so high that I could almost touch the banner that Tío Gabriel had painted. It said "**Feliz** Eid" in green, white, and **rojo**. I asked Abuela if he was named after the Angel Jibreel.

She nodded and rewarded me by letting me be the first to sit down for breakfast.

The food was set up in the dining room for the grown ups and in the backyard for the **niños**. Tía Marta cooked most of the food. She told me that she had made my favorite **empanadas**.

They were filled with **pollo** and cheese. She also made: tacos with eggs and **papas**, black beans, guacamole, and churros.

After eating our breakfast, my cousins and I drank our **leche** before having any cupcakes. I had already changed out of my Eid dress to keep it crumb-free.

When we finished our meal we counted our teeth. Jose, who is ten, had just lost his last baby tooth.

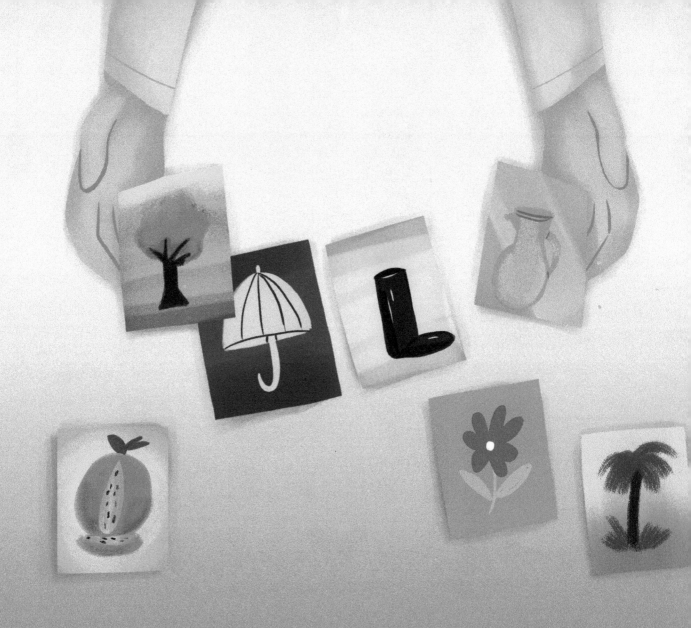

Since he is the oldest, Jose got to choose a game
for us to play. He chose lotería, which is like bingo,
but is played with pictures instead of números.

Jose already knew that his **nombre** was Spanish for Joseph. When I told him that in Arabic it is Yusuf, he felt special about having such a popular name.

He and the rest of my cousins wanted to learn more Arabic. Two Arabic **palabras** were added to their **vocabulario**. I taught them through a song. It goes, "Haleeb, leche, milk... Ma', agua, water."

After some more singing we gathered for a group **fotografía**.

When I got back home I printed the photo and added it to my scrapbook to remember this great día.

My **familia** had a wonderful gathering at Abuela's house. It was fun to be with Mama's family while celebrating Eid. Maybe next year they can all visit us for the first days of Ramadan.

Glossary + Arabic Words

año	year	عام (aam)
agua	water	ماء (ma')
abuela	grandmother	جدة (jadda)
avión	airplane	طائرة (ta'era)
cuchara	spoon	ملعقة (milaaqa)
bolsa	bag	كيس (kayss)
buenos días	good morning	صباح الخير (sabah alkhayr)
ropa	clothes	ملابس (malabis)
amigos	friends	أصدقاء (asdiqa')
desayuno	breakfast	إفطار (iftar)
mis hijos	my children	أولادي (awlady)
casa	house	بيت (bayt)
tíos	uncles (mother's brothers)	أخوال (akhwal)
tías	aunts (mother's sisters)	خالات (khalat)
tres	three	ثلاثة (thalatha)
feliz Eid	happy Eid	عيد سعيد (eid saeed)
rojo	red	أحمر (ahmar)
niños	children	أطفال (atfal)
empanadas	pies	فطائر (fata'ir)
pollo	chicken	دجاج (dajaj)
papas	potatoes	بطاطس (batatis)
leche	milk	حليب (haleeb)
lotería	bingo	بنغو (binghu)
números	numbers	أرقام (arqam)
nombre	name	إسم (ism)
palabras	words	كلمات (kalimat)
vocabulario	vocabulary	مفردات (mufradat)
fotografía	photograph	صورة (soora)
día	day	يوم (yawm)
familia	family	عائلة (aa'ila)

The Author:
Mariam Saad was raised in Southern California by Egyptian parents. She has a Bachelor of Arts in Business Administration from California State University, Fullerton. She worked at the family business for many years, with schools locally, and taught 8th Grade English abroad. With the birth of her son, her time and energy were focused at home while she surrounded him with reading materials and developmental toys. Before getting a taste for his board books, her son had taken interest in listening to her voice while he admired the images and felt the textures on the pages. This was the start of her inspiration in entering the world of children through story telling and lesson teaching.

The Illustrator:
Chaymaa Sobhy is a children's book illustrator based in Cairo, Egypt.